END(

This book titled "The Wealthy Home" is an analytical and probing approach to delving into your family's history to find the hidden story of success, faith, and promise locked in the generations that came before you. There are brilliant nuggets of hope, potential, and wealth in the capacity of your family tree that must be quarried. The insightful words in this book are from a source higher than the imagination and intellect of man. The concepts are confirmed by the oldest and most widely read book called the Bible. I see the fingerprints of the Creator in the writings of this book. The deoxyribonucleic acid (DNA) from the generations ("generate a nation") of our families have been waiting for this book to be written. Seize the opportunity now to say, "Hi to Your Family's Story"! This riveting book will inspire you to search your own family for answers concerning the hopes and dreams that you have never shared. I recommend this book to everyone regardless of your nationality, race, or station in life. If you were ever wondering about how to fulfill your purpose in life, read this book, it is a must!"

—Dr. Michael Laws / Nana Sufahen Kwasi
Bentum
Founder and Moreh of Beit Ephraim
Assembly
Author of A 7-day Journey: Insight into the
Biblical feasts

"The Wealthy Home is an excellent read for anyone seeking to build Biblical wealth. Adewunmi does an amazing job as he unfolds that wealth is more than our possessions. I was impacted by the importance of knowing and sharing your story. He does a great job as he takes us on a journey of unfolding the importance of searching and looking at our history, past, present, and future as it pertains to building wealth for today and legacy for tomorrow. Get ready as you embark on a journey to say, "Hi to your Story". You will not only be inspired but empowered through new knowledge and principles that are easy to apply to your family life. Jesus came to give us life and that more abundantly. Understanding Biblical wealth will help you live a more focused life. Thank you Adewunmi for your heart to change a generation."

—Apostle Tonya Roberson
Founder of Tonya Roberson Ministries.
Host of Life on Purpose broadcast and Fresh Wind gathering.
https://www.tonyarobersonministries.com/

"The Wealthy Home by Adewunmi Gbogboade combines the ancient wisdom of Torah, the Hebrew language and African wisdom to offer timeless and practical advice on how to build true generational wealth - both material wealth and spiritual wealth. Anyone interested in how to build righteous generations while breaking generational curses of lack should read this work."

—Apostle Onleilove Chika Alston
Founder of Prophetic Whirlwind Ministries.
Author of Prophetic Whirlwind: Uncovering
the Black Biblical Destiny.
https://propheticwhirlwind.com/

"When people think of wealth, they compartmentalize it most times to material wealth. But there is so much more to wealth than what we can see with our eyes or touch with our hands. Psalm 145:4 declares that "One generation will tell of your works to another." This implies the impartation of the spiritual reality of wealth, which is built from one generation to the next. Wealth of experience, wisdom, strength, the knowledge of God and the power to prosper in every way including financially. Adewunmi has written a book which unlocks the truths of prosperity and wealth from a unique and creative perspective for you and your entire bloodline. Be enriched and empowered as you delve into the treasure trove you hold in your hands."

—Benjamin Deitrick
Author of New Breed Arising

THE WEALTHY HOME

Building a foundation for Increase

Adewunmi Gbogboade

For enquiries and feedback, please email:
hebraicwisdom@gmail.com

Editors: Ademola A. Abodunrin and Ayodele Gbogboade

Cover Design: Corona Intl concepts

Publisher: G Publishing LLC

ISBN: 978-1-7366387-6-7

Library of Congress Control Number: 2022900966

Published and Printed in the United States of America

The emphasis on scripture is the author's addition. Please note that the author's style is to use Yahweh for the LORD.

DEDICATION

To my parents

Gbadewole and Azuka Gbogboade.

Your journey is now our journey. Your story will be told to generations yet unborn. Your roots are mighty in the earth. Many will rise and call you blessed. You have built a Wealthy Home.

ACKNOWLEDGEMENTS

I stand today as a product of so many people's efforts. A lot of people have sown into my life. Your roots run deep. I stand as a testament to the efforts of my parents, grandparents, great-grandparents and distant ancestors on my father's and mother's side. I acknowledge all that you did to pave the way for me. Also, I want to thank all the people that have privately and/or publicly affected my journey positively.

To my immediate family, thank you for helping me become the person that has authored this book. To my wife, Ayodele, words cannot express how much you have done and how grateful I am for you. You have built a wealthy home with your own hands. Generations yet unborn will rise and call you blessed. You are the embodiment of the things written in this book. You have created a wealthy home for others to model. To Israel, Adeyemi and Adeola, future generations will reference the foundation that you have created. Your sons and daughters will be mighty in the earth. Nations will serve you; kings and queens will bow down to you.

To Apostle Tonya Roberson, thank you for being a listening ear. Your wise counsel has helped form this message. Nine years ago, you said to me "stay the course". Over the years, you have listened, encouraged, guided, and supported me on my journey. You are a gift to the Body. I appreciate you.

To Femi Akande, words cannot express how grateful I am for all that you have done in my life. You fathered a generation while I was on campus in Lagos, Nigeria. You taught me and others by opening your home and your life. You became a father to a generation. This day we rise and call you blessed. You taught me timeless words of wisdom for family and economics. For over twenty years you have mentored and instructed me with timely words of wisdom. Thank You.

To Dr. Bernardine W. Daniels - who I fondly call "Bishop", thank you for writing the foreword of this book. Your story is our story. You inspire me to dig more in the scriptures, to reach higher in the heavens and to live better as commanded in the scriptures. You inspire me to press towards the mark of the high calling. Thank you for watching and encouraging me on this path. Your words of wisdom inspire me to learn the ways of Yahweh.

To Ann Parker, thank you for encouraging and supporting me. You believed in me when very few people did. You took a chance on me. Generations will rise and call you blessed.

To Barbara Yoder, the Apostle, thank you for creating an atmosphere for me to flourish. You labored in the 90s to bring racial reconciliation to the Detroit metro area. You led various teams to labor in intercession for my people in the city. You have built a house on a solid foundation. Full of history and richness. The stones are a testament to your labors. Thank you for helping me on my journey.

To Benjamin Deitrick, called to be an Apostle, thank you for laboring in the kingdom. You are building on the rich history of those that have gone ahead of us. We honor them by going further.

To Dr. Onelilove Chika Alston, the Apostle, and my Rosh Chodesh family. Y'all literally trolled me to get this done - you know who you are. I will return the favor my trolling y'all. Thank you for all your love, support, and encouragement. I will continue to return the favor by provoking each of you to good works. We will lend to many nations.

To Akindele Akinyemi, you braved the odds to form the Global African Business Association (GABA). You have not labored in vain. Generations yet unborn will rise and call you blessed.

To Dr. Michael Laws, a father not only in words but in deeds. I am grateful for your mentorship. You inspire me to learn more about our culture, our history, the Hebrew language and most especially the scriptures. Your labors have not been in vain. Thank you for accepting the apology to forgive my ancestors for selling your ancestors into slavery. Now Joseph must reveal himself to his brothers and become a united family. Our houses will be restored as it was in the beginning. The foundation for many generations is being laid.

My editorial team: Ayo and Ademola, thank you for fine-tuning and polishing this book.

TABLE OF CONTENTS

FOREWORD

Conversations with my father are never dull. At Ninety-three years young, born during the depression, his stories are rich with color, humor, and southern charm. He is one of the oldest of twenty children, fourteen boys and six girls, which included five sets of twins. He likes to tell the story of how my grandmother would present him, as a newborn, to visiting neighbors. Then take him back to the crib and bring him out again, showing him twice *(instead of his twin sister)* because he claims, he was *a better-looking baby* than her. His favorite topic of *'family reflections'* concerns my paternal great grandmother, his grandmother, affectionately called Ma'Rose.

Rosie King, born Rosie Star, Cherokee Nation and African American, was widely known and appreciated for being a mid-wife, medicine woman and caretaker of all who bore ailments. Riding in the dark on horseback, carrying her black bag, she facilitated the birth of countless babies into this world, including nineteen of her twenty grandchildren. There are amazing stories of storms and births, being paid in food, gathering medicines from the woods, pride, prejudice, and fierce determination. Ma'Rose never lost one baby! My father absolutely adored his grandmother and is convinced that, if she were still alive, none of his personal ailments would persist because Ma'Rose would know the cure! She was a legend in the counties she served, amongst both black and white southerners.

My paternal grandfather, Ralph Wormley, was a sharecropper, the son of Albert & Kittie. Poor, hardworking, noble, devoted to God, wife, children, and family. Both Ralph and Millie *(Ma'Roses' daughter, my incredible paternal grandmother, who birthed, nurtured, and cared for twenty babies)* instilled in their children the same work and faith ethics that would be handed down to more than one hundred and twenty-four grandchildren.

On August 4th, 2010, I purchased a subscription to an ancestry site and took the DNA test in search of more information regarding the wonderfully diverse characters that comprised my family tree. I was really looking for me. *Who am I? Why am I the way that I am?* Oftentimes for African Americans, the deep roots of our family trees and the wealth of heritage they convey, have been cut off by systemic racism and the institution of slavery. Still, I wanted to see who and what I could find and how it informs who I am today. I searched for any nuggets that may have been buried in family history that could help me, my children, grandchildren, and beyond, to know who we are. Comparing the DNA to my father's stories, I discovered buried in my roots: West Africa *(Nigeria 46%, Cameroon 23%, Benin, Togo, Senegal, Mali at 18%)* and of course the 13% European DNA of slave holders, namely Scotland, Ireland, and Germanic peoples. This completely redefined my concept of race and personal history, shedding light upon the riches expressed through me. We are so much more than we know.

Adewunmi Gbogboade, in The Wealthy Home, captures this revelation of self-knowledge and shows us how to build a foundation for true increase by looking back to look forward. He exhorts the reader to consider the wisdom intricately deposited in our family root structures, discovering the treasure hidden in our DNA. As you journey with him through this book, you will unlock wisdom and capture the true meaning of *'numbering your days'* through family history. Grab a journal, pen, and the stories of your family, and begin to sow and save their truths as precious seeds for the generations that will follow you to uncover and harvest! There *is* a message in your bloodline, a story implanted by your Creator, waiting to be uncovered, gathered, heard, and crafted in sharing, for the purpose of designing WEALTHY HOMES!

What does your tree look like? Where do the branches take you? What does the root structure supply to your life and how does it advise your purpose and destiny? If you don't know the answers to these questions, don't despair. You hold in your hand a tool that will guide you along the way. It's not too late, never too early, you still have time.

Thank you, Daddy, for the stories of Ma'Rose and all that her legacy supplies.

Thank you, Adewunmi, for your vision, prophetic revelation, and exhortation to go deeper because it really does matter!

Blessings to you dear reader, as you undertake this journey. May your efforts unveil the WEALTHY HOME the Lord your God has so generously given for a successful future!

—Bernardine Wormley Daniels,
Great-granddaughter of Ma'Rose King
Granddaughter of Ralph and Millie Wormley
Daughter of McArthur and Ida Wormley

The Wealthy Home

Mentorship is the dealership of knowledge that is available to you; the outcome of your choices is totally yours since mentorship also endears you to take responsibility. ~ iPen'21

> *Proverbs 13:22*
> *A good man leaves an inheritance to his children's children: and the **wealth** of the sinner is laid up for the just. (KJV)*

During one of my sessions teaching on Hebraic Wisdom for Investors via video conferencing, I made this statement to the group, "**You are wealthier than you think**". Many instantly thought about their bank accounts to connect with the statement. This is a very typical response irrespective of where you live. Nations are also categorized as "wealthy" nations and "poor" nations based on monetary values. We think in terms of money based on how wealth is defined and portrayed. Once you believe that we are not wealthy or that your home is not wealthy, you destroy the very foundation upon which resources can flow into the family.

> According to Psalm 11:3:
> *If the foundations be destroyed, what can the righteous do? (KJV)*

Every year in the United States, Fortune and

Forbes magazine publish a list of the "wealthiest" people in the world. This "wealth" is measured by certain criteria like assets. People on this list according to the magazine have acquired "wealth" and are celebrated for their "achievements". Hence, the drive to be "wealthy" or acknowledged as being "wealthy" is on the mind of a lot of people. Does the Fortune or Forbes list really define who is wealthy and who is not? Indeed, people that have exerted their effort to produce value resulting in the accumulation of possessions should be acknowledged and celebrated.

According to the Webster dictionary, wealth can be defined as follows:
1. The abundance of valuable material possessions or resources.
2. Abundant supply.
3. All property that has a money value or an exchangeable value.
4. All material objects that have economic utility especially the stock of useful goods having economic value in existence at any one time.

The above definitions give a picture of wealth as the accumulation of possessions or what you can tangibly see. Wealth is much more than an accumulation of possession or material things. However, the fruit or product of wealth is the accumulation of possession. Let us look at the scriptures to get a better understanding of the concept of **wealth**.

Hebraically, there is a difference between "riches" and "wealth". The first time the word wealth is shown in the scriptures is in the book of Genesis.

Genesis 34:29.

*"And all their **wealth**, and all their little ones, and their wives took they captive, and spoiled even all that was in the house". (KJV)*

The passage in Genesis shows wealth as material possession which includes riches.

Psalm 112:2-3

*"His seed shall be mighty upon earth: the generation of the upright shall be blessed. **Wealth** and riches shall be in his house: and his righteousness endures forever". (KJV)*

The passage in Psalms gives a distinction between wealth and riches. These words are used interchangeably in scripture, but they mean different things. Wealth in scripture is the building block for riches. Riches are the result of wealth. The Tanach (Hebrew scriptures) popularly known as the Old Testament of the bible was written in ancient Hebrew. This is also called paleo Hebrew. Ancient Hebrew language is pictorial in nature. Every picture has a numerical value and sound associated with it. To understand the word "wealth" in scriptures, we need to look at the ancient Hebrew picture. This can be found by looking at Strong's concordance word for "wealth".

Below is a picture of Gen 34:29 from biblehub.com interlinear bible:

Genesis 34 - Click for Chapter

802 [e]	853 [e]	2945 [e]	3605 [e]	853 [e]	2428 [e]	3605 [e]	853 [e]
nə-šê-hem,	wə-'eṯ-	ṭap-pām	kāl-	wə-'eṯ-	ḥê-lām	kāl-	wə-'eṯ- 29
וְשֵׁיהֶם	וְאֶת ,	טַפָּם	־כָּל	וְאֶת ,	חֵילָם	־כָּל	־וְאֶת 29
their wives	and	their little ones	all	and	their wealth	all	And
N-fpc | 3mp	Conj-w | DirObjM	N-msc | 3mp	N-msc	Conj-w | DirObjM	N-msc | 3mp	N-msc	Conj-w | DirObjM

1004 [e]	834 [e]	3605 [e]	853 [e]	962 [e]	7617 [e]
bab-bā-yiṯ.	'ă-šer	kāl-	wə-'êṯ	way-yā-ḇōz-zū;	šā-ḇū
בַּבָּיִת:	אֲשֶׁר	־כָּל	וְאֵת	וַיָּבֹזּוּ ,	שָׁבוּ
in the houses	that [was]	all	even	and they plundered	they took captive
Prep-b, Art | N-ms	Pro-r	N-msc	Conj-w | DirObjM	Conj-w | V-Qal-ConsecImperf-3mp	V-Qal-Perf-3cp

The words written in black in the picture above were written in the Masoretic text or the modern Hebrew. This was the writing style during Yahshua (Jesus) time. The paleo - Hebrew pictures precede this writing style. This writing style added vowels to the ancient Hebrew writing for pronunciations. The scriptures that we read today in English were translated from modern Hebrew and many words were added to them or mistranslated. To understand the scriptures, we must go to the original writings. The Bible was written in the Hebrew language, with the Hebrew culture in mind.

Conducting a search of H2428 through the King James Version of the bible, you will see different interpretations connected with the word Chayil or wealth. Some of the interpretations are as follows:

- Wealth

20

- Host
- Activity
- Army
- Able
- Valiantly
- Estate
- Strength

These interpretations paint a picture that wealth is much more than possessions. The translators of the King James Bible used different words in different passages to explain the concept of wealth. None of it has to do with money. It has more to do with the building blocks of value. The King James Version of the Bible was translated from the Hebrew language. At the time that the Bible was written, the writing style was in pictures called Paleo-Hebrew. This writing style resembles the Egyptian hieroglyphs that are seen today on ancient Egyptian structures. Each alphabet has a picture that captures the meaning of the alphabet or word.

The Strong's number for wealth is H2428. The root word is Chayil. The Paleo-Hebrew root is Chet 𐤇 and Lamed 𐤋

- Chet 𐤇 has a numerical value of 8. Among other things, it represents:
  - A fence
  - A wall
  - Protection
  - Outside
  - To surround

- To guard

Pictorially, it looks like a fence.

- Lamed ל has a numerical value of 30. Among other things, it stands for:
  - Authority
  - Control
  - Direction
  - Yoke

Pictorially, it looks like a shepherd's staff.

ל‌ח has the following meanings:
- Wall authority
- Outside walk
- Surround walk
- Outside authority

I like to use the last definition: Outside authority. This connotes something that is used to "protect and defend". This is the concept of accumulated value/assets over time. You can also come up with your own definition using the definitions of Chet and Lamed above. I encourage you to write your own definition and come up with two or three scriptures that explain your definition. Feel free to email your thoughts to hebraicwisdom@gmail.com.

A deeper look at wealth shows a root that is linked with the following:
1. Education - Knowledge of natural occurrences.
2. Experience - Application of education to problem-solving.

22

3. Purpose - Understanding the functionality of something.
4. Wisdom - Ability to solve problems.
5. Value creation - Extracting purpose from something.

In other words, what one has mastered or gained mastery in, is acknowledged outside the house. These skills are gotten in the home. These skills are honed and used to solve problems outside the home. When this happens, resources start to flow to the home or to the members of the home. These resources are for the advancement of the home.

Definition of a Wealthy Home
A wealthy home is a home that harnesses the wisdom imbedded within its rich history to empower each member of the family to solve problems within their sphere of influence.

Important points to note about the wealth home:
- A wealthy home is a home that intentionally creates an enabling environment for all its members to be productive.
- Value creation is at the core of the wealthy home.
- The wealthy home is constantly looking at passing wealth to the third generation. The most experienced (patriarchs/matriarchs) members of the family teach the least experienced members of the family (children under fifteen).

Adding the numerical value of Lamed *J* and Chet

III, We get thirty-eight. Based on that, I have concluded that at age thirty-eight, a person should have proven certain levels of mastery to have "outside authority" or "wealth". Most people consider forty as "middle age" or "mid-life". In fact, there is an English idiom, "a fool at forty is a fool forever". Meaning, "someone who reaches middle age and continues to act foolishly is unlikely to start acting more maturely".[1]

It is interesting that if you observe the world around you, you will always come to a scriptural conclusion on any subject matter. The Torah, the earth, and the heavens are always in agreement. They agree as one. According to Deuteronomy 19:15: "...At the mouth of two witnesses, or at the mouth of three witnesses, shall the matter be established". Once you realize that you are wealthy, the next step in the process is to understand how to intentionally build the foundation of a wealthy home that lasts for generations yet unborn.

> Proverbs 13:22
> *A good man leaves an inheritance to his children's children: and the **wealth** of the sinner is laid up for the just. (KJV)*

Below is a picture of Proverbs 13:22 from biblehub.com interlinear bible:

◀ **Proverbs 13:22** ▶

Proverbs 13 - Click for Chapter

6662 [e]	6845 [e]	1121 [e]	1121 [e]	5157 [e]	2896 [e]
laṣ·ṣad·dîq,	wə·ṣā·p̄ūn	bā·nîm;	bə·nê-	yan·ḥîl	ṭō·wḇ,
לַצַּדִּיק	וְצָפוּן ,	בָּנִים	בְּנֵי־	יַנְחִיל	טוֹב 22
for the righteous	but is stored up	children	of his children	leaves an inheritance to	A good [man]
Prep-l, Art | Adj-ms	Conj-w | V-Qal-QalPassPrtcpl-ms	N-mp	N-mpc	V-Hifil-Imperf-3ms	Adj-ms

2398 [e]	2428 [e]
ḥō·w·ṭê.	ḥêl
חוֹטֵא׃ .	חֵיל
of the sinner	the wealth
V-Qal-Prtcpl-ms	N-msc

The above passage of scripture can be interpreted/re-written as this:

> Proverbs 13:22
> *A functional person passes down continuous wealth (education, experience, purpose, wisdom, value creation) to his children's children. The wealth (education, experience, purpose, wisdom, value creation) of the sinner is stored for the upright.*

You are wealthier than you think. You belong to a Wealthy Home.

Thoughts to consider:
- Wealth is not measured in the accumulation of assets but in the accumulation of experiences.
- Your home is filled with a lot of experiences.
- Age thirty-eight reflected an ago that one

25

should have accumulation proper knowledge of life experiences.
- Inheritance is wealth passed to the next generation.
- It is time to build a Wealthy Home.

Chapter One

History: Say Hi to your Story

H istory always comes with an opportunity to rewrite it. ~ iPen'21

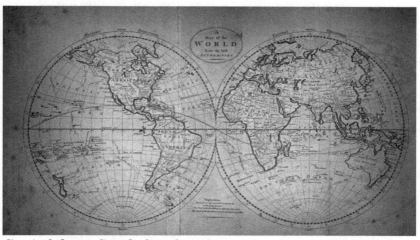

Copied from Stock freedom.[2]

> Psalm 90:12
> *"So, **teach us to number our days,** that we may apply our hearts unto wisdom." (KJV)*
> Psalm 90: 12

> *"So, make us know **how to assign our days,** that we may come to a heart of wisdom." (CLV)*

"Teach us to number our days" is an interesting part of scripture. According to the psalmist, the prerequisite to gaining a heart of wisdom is in numbering your days. What does it mean to number days? The concept of numbering your days has to do with keeping an account of what has happened in the past. An example of this was when Pharaoh asked Jacob (Ya'akov) how old he was.

> Genesis 47: 8-9
> *Pharaoh asked Ya 'akov, how old are you? and Ya 'akov replied, "The time of my stay on earth has been one hundred and thirty years; they have been few and difficult, fewer than the years my ancestors lived." (Complete Jewish Bible).*

In the passage above, His response was the years of his pilgrimage/journey and that of his fathers. The present is always connected to the past. The fruit is an extension of the root. This is where history comes in.

The Merriman-Webster dictionary defines history as the following:
1. A tale or a story.
2. A chronological record of significant events (such as those affecting a nation or institution), often including an explanation of their causes.
3. A branch of knowledge that records and explains past events.
4. Events of the past.

These definitions give us insight into what we understand as history. However, history can be defined through the actual word itself.

The word "**HISTORY**" can be broken into two - "**Hi**" and "**Story**". The word "**Hi**" is a form of greeting or salutation, expressing delight at seeing someone or acknowledging the existence of someone. The word "**Story**" acknowledges a series of events that have happened or is to happen. The combination of **"Hi"** and **"Story"** gives us a picture of the word History.

"**History**" or "**Number of days**" can be defined or understood as the following:
- An acknowledgment of the existence of a series of events.
- A salutation or call to attention of what has happened or is about to happen.

Our present reflects our history. This in turn gives a reflection of our future. History is always bound to repeat itself. Say "**Hi**" to your "**story**".

You have a story to tell. Your family is a story that is being told to the world. You may feel like you do not have a story to tell but I want you to know that you are part of a story that has been told. Say "Hi" to your "story". Acknowledge your story. Hear the call to look again at your story. Life as we know it today started from somewhere in the distant past. You are a product of your history. This history, however good or bad, needs to be acknowledged. There is a story that is unfolding through your life, deeply embedded in the root system of your family structure. This story is a continuation of a story that started at a point in your family tree.

Many people do not know anything or know very little about their family history. If that, is you, do not worry, NOW is the time to say "**Hi (acknowledge, then salute)**" to your "**Story**"? You will be surprised at what you find. The journey to building your family tree can be a long and tedious one. This can be synonymous with studying the root system of a big tree. You may know a few things about your family, but you will need to go beyond the surface to dig into the root system to find the source of your "wealth". This process is ongoing. You cannot exhaust the number of stories, wisdom, and knowledge that you will find from your family root system.

The structure of your family is like a tree. We often use the phrase "family tree". Your history is at the root of the tree. The depth of the tree's roots gives a picture of how tall and/or strong the tree is in the forest. As you put together your family tree, you will observe a "huge taproot". This root system runs down very deep in families. Strong families have roots that run down very deep.

For example, a certain relative was born in the distant past. That relative had children, possibly did XYZ, and passed on. You sometimes look at a story like that and say, "there is nothing significant about the story of that person". On the surface, there might not be anything significant about that relative, your parents, or grandparents. However, my hope and prayer is that when you are done reading this book you will find inspiration to look at your story differently. The roots of our family genealogy can be likened to the root system of a tree. These root systems hold vital nutrients for the tree to blossom and thrive. We have a lot to glean from our root systems.

In her article, "Answers in the trees", Kate Ekhator stated: "Trees save nearly 400 billion gallons of stormwater annually by retaining a percentage of the precipitation through their leaf system. In addition, the root structure also helps in **holding another percentage of the precipitation.** Furthermore, those same root structures create **preferential pathways** that increase infiltration capacity of soils."[3]

In their article, "Healthy Roots and Healthy Trees," J.M. Sillick and W.R. Jacobi stated: "The root system of a tree performs many vital functions. In winter, it is a **storehouse for essential food reserves** needed by the tree to produce spring foliage. **Roots absorb and transport water and minerals** from the soil to the rest of the tree. **Roots also anchor the portion** of the tree above ground. It is important to keep the portion above ground healthy to ensure an adequate food supply for the roots to continue their important functions."[4]

A summary of the root function from the articles above are as follows:
- Roots hold a portion of precipitation.
- Roots create preferential pathways.
- Roots are storehouses for essential food reserves.
- Roots transport water and nutrients.
- Roots are the anchor of the tree.

Our family tree begins with its root system. This root system has the following characteristics:
- It is full of precipitation. The word precipitation denotes the concept of "to precipitate". It speaks of the presence of moisture. Moisture Hebraically speaks of freshness. There is a lot of fresh wisdom to

31

glean from our patriarchs and matriarchs. There is much wisdom in our roots.

- It has preferential pathways. This speaks of the nature (behavior) and career of the offspring. I will go into more detail in chapter three. There is much wisdom in our roots.
- It has storehouses for essential food reserves. Deep within our family tree are stories of survival and overcoming. How did our patriarchs and matriarchs overcome in the past? There is much wisdom in our roots.
- It transports water and nutrients. This speaks of the ability to nurture. Our patriarchs and matriarchs are always looking for ways to nurture the next generation. There is much wisdom in our roots.

Proverbs 3:13-18
*Happy is the man who finds wisdom, and the man who gains hold of comprehension. For her merchandise is better than merchandise of silver, and her income than fine gold. She is more precious than rubies so that all your desires are not equal to her. Length of days are in her right hand, and in her left hand are riches and glory. Her ways are ways of pleasantness, and all her tracks are peace. **She is a tree of life to those holding fast to her**, and those upholding her will be made happy.* (CLV)

- The root system is an anchor. This speaks of stability, strength, and fortitude. The ability to STAND the test of time. Our patriarchs and matriarchs have a lot of instructions on standing firm on what we believe in. A lot of these teachings are embedded in their life stories. There is much wisdom in our roots.

To gain a heart of wisdom - to get inspiration on how to solve problems, we have to say **Hi** (acknowledge, then salute) to our **story**. You need to look back to look forward. There is much wisdom in our roots.

Thoughts to consider:
- Have you created and documented your family tree?
- If yes, have you documented your family stories?
- If yes, have you highlighted the wisdom in the stories to help your move forward?
- If yes, are your prepared to handle situations based on the wisdom that you have gleaned from your family stories?
- It is time to Build a Wealthy Home.

Chapter Two

Generate-a-nation

H istory is the summary of our limitations since the future is an epitome of boundless possibilities. ~ iPen'21

A drawing of Benin City was made by a British officer in 1897.[5]

> Deuteronomy 5:9
> *You shall not bow yourself down to them, nor be made to serve them, for I, Yahweh (The LORD) your Elohim (God), am a jealous El, visiting the depravity of the fathers on the sons, on the third and on the fourth generation, to those hating Me.* (CLV)

You may say "I do not tell my story because it is full of pain", but I want to assure you that you have a story to tell. Your story is worth telling, and it speaks of a good and expected end. Your family also has a story to tell. Your story is waiting to be acknowledged by you first. There is a lot of hope in your story. There is a lot of wisdom in your family's story that is waiting to be unlocked for the world to see. I want to call your attention to a story that began possibly four generations before you. There is much wisdom in our roots.

Some questions to consider are as follows:
- What is your story?
- What is the series of events in the distant past that has defined your family?
- What is the series of events in the near past and present that is defining your family?
- What is the series of events in the future that will define your family?

Your story starts with you. You are part of an unfolding story. Your family is part of an unfolding story. You may be asking yourself the following questions:
1. Do I have a story?
2. What does my story sound like?
3. Is my story worth telling?
4. What does my story mean?

Before you start the exercise of looking into your story, you need to know how many preceding generations you are to review. Let us look at the word "generation".

The Merriman-Webster dictionary defines the word "generation" as follows:
1. The average span of time between the birth of parents and that of their offspring.
2. A body of living beings constituting a single step in the line of descent from an ancestor.[6]

These definitions paint a picture of pro-creation from an ancestor. Taking a deeper look at the word "generation", it can be broken into three parts: **"generate-a-nation"**.

Well, that puts things in a whole new light. It sounds like a portion of scripture in Isaiah.

> Isaiah 60:22:
> *A little one shall become a thousand, and a small one a strong nation: I Yahweh (The LORD) will hasten it in his time.* (CLV)

Let us turn our attention to the Hebraic understanding of the word "generation". The first place that the word "generations" was mentioned in the scripture was in Genesis 2:4. *"These are the generations of the heavens and of the earth when they were created, on the day that the Lord God made the earth and the heavens".* (KJV)

> Genesis 2:4
>
> *These are the chronological records of the heavens and the earth when they were created, in the day that Yahweh the Elohim made earth and heavens* (CLV)

To understand the Hebraic word for generation, we need to look at the strong concordance reference number H8435. The word is "to-led-aw". The paleo Hebrew root is Lamed ✓ and Dalet ⊓

- Lamed ✓ has a numerical value of 30. It represents among other things:
  - Authority
  - Control
  - Direction
  - Yoke
  - Pictorially, it looks like a shepherd's staff.
- Dalet ⊓ has a numerical value of 4. It represents, among other things:
  - A door
  - A pathway
  - To enter
  - The back-and-forth movement
  - Pictorially, it looks like a door.

✓ ⊓ has the following meanings:
- The door of authority
- The pathway to authority
- Enter the walk
- The authority that moves back and forth

Hebraically, we can define a generation as that authority that moves back and forth. This gives us the idea of the one that wealth (education, experience, purpose, wisdom, value creation) is being passed to. The best picture to capture this is that of passing the baton in a relay race. The baton has been passed to you. It is time to run the race set before you and extend the tent pegs of your family. Every generation or generated nation would need to learn from those that have gone ahead of them for the wealthy family to flourish. Has a nation been generated in your family? Adding the numerical value of Lamed ל and Dalet ד We get 34. Based on that, I have concluded that a generation represents thirty-four years.

In 2005 Devine, D wrote in the article "How long is a generation?" that "Biological anthropologist Agnar Helgeson and colleagues used the Icelandic deCODE genetics database to arrive at a female line interval of 28.12 years for the most recent generations and 28.72 years for the whole lineage length. Male line lineages showed a similar difference—31.13 years for the recent generations and 31.93 years overall. For a more mathematically appealing average, Helgason and fellow researchers recommended estimating female generational line intervals at 30 years and male generational intervals at 35 years, based on the Quebec and Iceland studies."[7]

In 2016, Devine, D wrote in "How long is a generation? Science provides an answer" that for the time being, given the imprecision of the various results and his own need for an estimate that lends itself to easy calculation, he used three generations per century (33 years each) for male lines, three and half generations per century or seven in two centuries (29 years each) for female lines whenever he needed to convert generations into years. As a check on those values, which were based on extensive data and rigorous mathematical analysis; although rounded off for ease of use, he decided to compare the generational intervals from all-male or all-female ranges in his own family lines for the years 1700 to 2000 and was pleasantly surprised to see how closely they agree. For a total of 21 male-line generations among five lines, the average interval was 34 years per generation. For 19 female-line generations from four lines, the average was 29 years per generation.[8]

Science always arrives at the same conclusions as they are written in the scriptures. Now that you understand what a generation is and how many years are in a generation, it is time to go back to four generations (generate-a-nation) to see what story has been unfolding in your family. If a generation is thirty-four years Hebraically and scientifically, then four generations are One hundred and thirty-six years. Do you have a hundred and thirty-six years of your family's history?

Say "Hi (acknowledge, then salute)" to your "Story"

How deep are you willing to go into your roots to find out details about your story? For your story to come alive, you will have to dig deep and wide. You will have to go below the surface of what you know, have heard about, or currently experiencing. A good place to start is to create a family tree by getting a genealogy software or a database. There are many good ones on the market. I personally use Roots Magic. To create a family tree, you start with yourself.

Document what you know and can remember about your life experiences. Then expand your documentation to your parents, grandparents, and great-grandparents.

After that, start expanding to uncles, aunts, cousins, nieces, and nephews. The goal of this exercise is to understand what they did and what they excelled in. Finding out how they excelled in what they excelled in is an excellent goal. How they excelled in what they excelled in is education. This education gotten over the years must be passed down from generation to generation. The next generation continues the story. You are a story that is in motion and the world is waiting to hear your story. Your story is that of overcoming many obstacles and many hurdles to push beyond the current circumstance of life.

Say "**Hi (acknowledge then salute)**" to your "**Story**"

The first generation produced children (second generation) then they produced children (third generation) and then they produced YOU (fourth generation). You can go as far as the tenth generation in your family tree to see what information you can collect from your father's side and your mother's side. The fourth generation is usually a good starting point. Embarking on this journey has opened my eyes to a lot of things in my family and my wife's family. A lot of questions that I had were answered by looking at the common trends in the family story. The scriptures below highlight a pattern in looking back at three or four generations.

Exodus 20:5
You shall not bow yourself down to them, nor be made to serve them, for I, Yahweh your Elohim,

am a jealous El, visiting the depravity of the fathers on the sons, on the third and on the fourth generation, to those hating me (CLV)

Numbers 14:18
Yahweh, slow to anger and with much benignity and truths, bearing with depravity and transgression and sins, yet He is not holding innocent, nay innocent, but is visiting the depravity of the fathers on the sons, on the third and on the fourth generation. (CLV)

Exodus 34:7
Preserving benignity to thousands, bearing with depravity, transgression, and sin, yet He is not holding innocent, nay innocent, but visiting the depravity of the fathers on the sons and on the sons' sons, on the third and on the fourth generation. (CLV)

Hebrews 7:5-10
And, indeed, those of the sons of Levi who obtain the priestly office have a direction to take tithes from the people according to the law, that is, their brethren, even those who also have come out of the loins of Abraham. Yet he who is not of their genealogy has tithed Abraham and has blessed him who has the promises. Now, beyond all contradictions, the inferior is blessed by the better. And here, indeed, dying men are obtaining tithes, yet there, one of whom it is attested that he is living. And so, I say that, through Abraham, Levi also, who is obtaining the tithes, has been tithed, for he was still in the

loins of his father when Melchizedek met with him. (CLV)

2 Timothy 1:5

Getting a reminder of the unfeigned faith, which is in you, which first makes its home in your grandmother Lois, and in your mother Eunice. Now, I am persuaded that it is in you also. (CLV)

The scripture references state that he visits the iniquity to the third and the fourth generation. In other words, the patterns from the third and fourth generations in the past hold true up till now. Therefore, it is important to look at least four generations in the family tree. The story of our patriarchs and matriarchs continues to play out today. Every fourth generation, an opportunity is presented to the family to re-write the family's story. If this opportunity is not acted on, the pattern in the family may continue for another three to four generations until someone comes along to change the course of the family's story.

You are about to rewrite the story of your family. This can be done by unlocking the wisdom buried in your roots. It is the concept of numbering the days of your family. I encourage you to go back four generations - one hundred and thirty-six years. What it was like with your ancestors is a clue to what it will be like in the future.

Some questions to think about:
1. How did my family overcome?
2. How did my family move: Geographically and socio-economically?

3. How did my family grow: Population (members) and social influence?

In the same vein, the actions that you show today would be as seeds for the third and fourth generations to harvest. When Abraham met Melchizedek, his great-grandson Levi was in his loins. Abraham gave tithes to Melchizedek (the seed was sown). Eight - ten generations later, Levi received tithes (the fruit of what was sown). The seeds that you are sowing today are setting up the third and/or fourth generation for a massive harvest. I encourage you to be intentional about your actions and how you respond to things around you. A nation is in your loins and nations will be generated from you.

What you do is documented in your blood and passed down to the next generation (generated nation). Be intentional about passing down what will build a wealthy HOME. In the future, you will also be referred to as a patriarch or matriarch of a nation. If you have not captured your history, Now is the time to start. Saying Hi to your story is quite easy and practical. At this time, I want to say "**Hi (acknowledge, then salute)**" to my "**Story**". Below is an example of how you can say Hi to your story. I would use my family as an example.

My family:

- On my father's paternal side, I want to acknowledge and salute my grandfather, Hon. L. Sanni Gbogboade, and his parents. He was very diligent and industrious. A man of integrity in every respect. He built a successful business trading in hides and skin (leather). He

43

left his home for another part of the country. In that place, he contested and won several local elections. He served serval terms as the chairman of the district council, councilor, and chairman of the final review committee among other positions/functions. He was actively involved in local politics leading up to the independence of Nigeria in 1960. He excelled as a local politician for several years and eventually became a kingmaker.

- On my father's maternal side, I want to acknowledge and salute my grandmother, Ajoke Gbogboade, and her parents. They raised her in the family business selling palm oil, fish, and household items. She learned how to trade from her mother and became remarkably successful in the business.

> *My paternal grandparents told my father a lot of stories on how our family overcame through a lot of adversity. He left a legacy of impacting the wisdom of diligence, valuing a good name (integrity) and entrepreneurship. Incidentally, my father became the regional director for a shoe manufacturing company in Nigeria. The entrepreneurship spirit was passed down to my father who built several businesses. My father has the keen eye to see business*

opportunities before it becomes mainstream. Recently, we were chatting about the next real estate location business frontier on the outskirts of Lagos. He recommended a location. Not up to six months, there was news of a major investment and development in that area. The wisdom passed down by our forebears have created a wealthy HOME. We would pay it forward for generations yet unborn.

- On my mother's paternal side, I want to acknowledge and salute my grandfather, Augustine Dumbili, and his parents. He came from humble beginnings and worked his way up to become a director in Bata Shoe company - a Canadian company with operations in Nigeria. He mentored a lot of young people during his time on earth. He funded research on leather production and consumption in the country.

- On my mother's maternal side, I want to acknowledge and salute my grandmother, Elizabeth Dumbili, and her parents. She was raised in the palace of the Kingdom of Aboh in Delta State, Nigeria. She left Aboh- her hometown in Delta State, came to Lagos with her aunt, and became a successful business-woman trading in fabrics.

My maternal grandparents raised my mother to be a pioneer. As pioneers themselves. My maternal grandfather educated the Nigerian public about eating healthy and wearing good shoes. Rising to the level of executive director, he pioneered the company's expansion to the western part of the country. My mother took on pioneering ocean fish farming projects and consulted for the United Nations. The wisdom passed down by our forebears have created a wealthy home. We would pay it forward for generations yet unborn.

My wife's family:

- On her father's paternal side, I want to acknowledge and salute her grandfather, Samuel Adeniyi Awosanya, and his parents. He was a valiant and courageous man. He was a soldier. He fought during World War II alongside fifteen thousand troops from Nigeria in Burma. He served in the 81st division of the then British army. In August 1944, the division re-entered the Kaladan valley, forcing the Japanese and Indian National Army to abandon Mowdok, a few miles east of the Indian/Burmese frontier. The division then advanced down the valley once again, reaching Myohaung near the mouth of the river on 28

46

January 1945. He was part of the 50,000 Nigerians alongside two million Africans that served in World War II. He returned home and retired on his farm.

- On her father's maternal side, I want to acknowledge and salute her grandmother, Mary Awosanya, and her parents. They raised her in the family business. She learned how to trade from her mother and became a merchant. She traded with people from various parts of the state and the nation.

> *Her paternal grandparents raised her father to be thorough, strong, and independent. Her father became an accomplished banker and he worked with the state and local governments to bring much needed resources to his hometown. As a solider in World War II, her grandfather fought for what he believed in, and he fought for others. He taught her father to do the same. My wife is passing on this ancient wisdom to our children. The wisdom passed down by our forebears have created a wealthy home. We would pay it forward for generations yet unborn.*

- On her mother's paternal side, I want to acknowledge and salute her grandfather Shoade "Ile-Laboye" Shokoya and his parents.

He came from humble beginnings in his hometown. He rose to become the head of all the hunters in the community. He was a successful hunter and farmer. He was also a chief in his town and a kingmaker.

- On her mother's maternal side, I want to acknowledge and salute her grandmother Sadat Shokoya and her parents. They raised her in the family business. She learned how to trade from her mother and became remarkably successful in the business.

> *Her maternal grandparents raised her mother to be independent and industrious. These traits are very evident in my wife's mother and her. As a single mother, my mother-in-law raised three children after the passing of her husband; she did this without any formal education beyond elementary school or office job. She tried her hands on different business opportunities. She started, built, and grew her business through some of the worst times in Nigeria's history. My mother-in-law financed the education of all her children by herself. The wisdom passed down by our forebears have created a wealthy HOME. We would pay it forward*

for generations yet unborn.

The next page is left bank for you to say "**Hi (acknowledge, then salute)**" to your "**Story**".

Chapter Three

The Message in the Blood

Any time there's an issue, there's an opportunity.
~ iPen'20

The Ethiopian Bible written in Ge'ez, an ancient dead language of Ethiopia, it's nearly 800 years older than the King James Version and contains 81-88 books compared to 66. It includes the Book of ENOCH, Esdras, Baruch, and all 3 Books of MACCABEE, and a host of others that were excommunicated from the KJV. Picture from Orthodox Christian Laity.[10]

Ecclesiastes 1:9
What occurred once, it shall occur again, and what was done, it shall be done again. There is nothing at all new under the sun. (CLV)

The world has evolved over the past few years. Empires have risen and fallen. Families have risen and fallen. However, you are still here. In other words, your family has overcome a lot of adversity. Your family has weathered through a lot of challenges. The experiences on how they overcame is recorded in the blood and passed down to the next generation. This courage is what is pumping through your veins. This courage is saying "I will overcome". I say to you, "You are an overcomer". Your family may still have scars from the battles that were fought in the near or distant past, but I want you to know that because you are alive today, you are an overcomer and will overcome every challenge that is ahead of you.

Ecclesiastes 9:4
"For to him that is joined to all the living there is hope: for a living dog is better than a dead lion."

Below is a summary of events that the world has experienced in the last one hundred and thirty years:
→ 1885 | The Congo was colonized by King Leopold II of Belgium, paving the way for genocide.
→ 1890 | Liliuokalani was proclaimed the last monarch and only queen regent of the Kingdom of Hawai'i.

51

→ 1900 | Humans began to generate potentially unstable climates. Temperatures, nudged up by emissions of greenhouse gases, rose sharply at the beginning of the 1900s, but wind patterns were largely unchanged, creating an unnatural combination of conditions. The two together created potentially greater instability in climate.

→ 1912 | Last emperor of China Puyi was forced to abdicate, Yuan Shikai became the first president.

→ 1916-1970 | The Great Migration was the relocation of more than 6 million African Americans from the rural South to the cities of the North, Midwest, and West from about 1916 to 1970.

→ 1919-1920 | European civilization (Italy/Britain/France) reached its peak. The Treaty of Versailles was established.

→ 1920-1945 | Global-scale wars.

→ 1945 | America rose. The atomic age was born to end the Second World War. India gained independence on August 15, 1947, after a 200-year British rule.

→ 1945-1991 | Cold War between America and Soviets.

→ 1948 | Universal Declaration of Human Rights adopted by the United Nations. The institution of apartheid in South Africa.

→ 1950-2000 | Air transportation led to global travel on an unprecedented scale.

→ 1957-1965 | Civil Rights movement in the United States brought down Jim Crow era laws. Dr Martin Luther King Jr gives the "I have a dream speech" in 1963. This speech has inspired millions. African nations gain independence from European colonialism. 27 African nations (50%) gain independence between 1951-1968. The OAU (Organization of African Unity) is founded by thirty-two African countries on May 25, 1963, in Addis Ababa, Ethiopia.

→ 1961 | First humans in space.
→ 1969 | First humans on a celestial body other than earth; an American reaches the moon.
→ 1973-1975 | Yom Kippur war. The global oil embargo.
→ 1975 | Human population: 4 billion.
→ 1980s | A period of transition in the fields of culture and the arts as many African countries grappled with the vicious cycles of nation building, moving from the promises of political independence to the nightmarish realism of the postcolonial.
→ 1991 | The Soviet Union collapsed.
→ 1994 | Apartheid ends in South Africa. Nelson Mandela becomes the first black president of South Africa.
→ 1995 | The internet electronically connects the globe.
→ 1999 | Africa's most populous nation - Nigeria returns to democracy after sixteen years of military rule since 1983. It was in a civil war from 1967- 1970.
→ 2000 | Human population: 6 billion. Widespread interbreeding between formerly

isolated peoples. Human genetic diversity began to decrease.

→ 2001 | Terrorists attacked America. America declared "War on Terror".

→ 2002 | Discovery of Rapid Climate Change: Only within the past decade have researchers warmed to the possibility of abrupt shifts in earth's climate. Sometimes, it takes a while to see what one is not prepared to look for. The OAU (Organization for African Unity) is dissolved and replaced with the African Union.

→ 2003 | The Chinese sent man to low earth orbit.

→ 2007-2008 | The global financial crisis.

→ 2008 | The United States elected the first black president- President Barak Obama.

→ 2010 - present | Clash of Civilizations: the pattern of conflict in a post-Cold War world.

→ 2019 (Dec) - present | Coronavirus pandemic.[9]

The events above shaped the world one way or the other. Your family might have been affected positively or negatively by these events. There are lots of stories from the past one hundred and thirty-six years in your family. The bottom line is - you are still here. Your ancestors overcame the difficulties in the world. Your family has walked through these events. Buried in your family history are nuggets to help the next generation (generated nation) overcome for the next one hundred and thirty-six years and beyond.

Josiah was a king in ancient Israel. Historians believe that he reigned in Judah from 640-610 BCE

(+/- 2yrs). He was credited with instituting a lot of reforms and turning the hearts of the people back to Yahweh (The LORD).

According to 2 Chronicles 35:18

"And there was no Passover like to that kept in Israel from the days of Samuel the prophet; neither did all the kings of Israel keep such a Passover as Josiah kept, and the priests, and the Levites, and all Judah and Israel that were present, and the inhabitants of Jerusalem".

Josiah's story begins hundreds of years (approximately two hundred years) before his birth.

According to 1 Kings 13:1-5 (CLV):

Verse 1: Behold, a man of Elohim, came from Judah by the word of Yahweh (The LORD) to Bethel while Jeroboam was standing on the altar to fume incense.

Verse 2: He called out against the altar by the word of Yahweh and said, O altar, altar, thus speaks Yahweh: Behold, a son shall be born to the house of David; Josiah is his name. And he will sacrifice on you the priests of the high places who are fuming incense on you, and he shall burn human bones on you.

Verse 3: Then he gave a miracle on that day, saying, this is the miracle of which Yahweh has spoken: Behold, the altar will be torn apart, and the greasy ash that is on it will be poured out.

Verse 4: Now this came to pass: As the king heard- the word of the man of Elohim that he had called out against the altar in Bethel,

Jeroboam stretched out his hand from above the altar, saying- Apprehend him! And his hand that he stretched out against him dried up so that he could not bring it back - to himself.

Verse 5: As for the altar, it was torn apart, and the greasy ash was poured out from the altar, according to the miracle that the man of Elohim had given by the word of Yahweh.

The picture below shows the genealogy of the kings of Israel and Judah. Based on a literal interpretation of 1st and 2nd Kings. Note: In the kings of Israel, a horizontal arrow can indicate a change of dynasty (lack of known genealogical connection).[12]

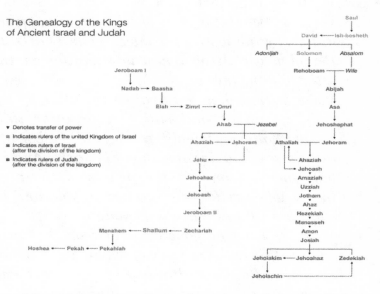

After the national word was proclaimed, "it" as a seed was sown into the bloodline of the kings waiting for the right atmospheric conditions for the fruit to manifest. The tree took years of forming strong root systems in the earth creating an enabling environment for the one that is to come. As it is for a nation, so it is for the family. The building block of any nation is the family. Are you the one that is to come in your family? There are prophecies waiting to be fulfilled in your family.

The elders of each family can look at each member of the family and tell what the child will become in the future. They can also look beyond the current generation into the third or tenth generation to speak about what will happen. These words spoken by elders in past generations are waiting for the branch that will plug into the root system.

Josiah may or may not have known about the prophecy spoken about him, but he fulfilled the word. What if he knew about it and he became very intentional about it? I believe that he would have done more. This word was specific by name (Josiah). However, most prophetic words in scripture are not as specific as this, that is, the indication of a name. As it is in scripture, so it is in your family. There is a prophecy in your bloodline that will be fulfilled through you. I am not sure about the environment that you have grown up in. You may not know the prophecies that you are fulfilling, but I want to assure you that if you become intentional about creating a wealthy HOME, your current and future family will be greater than the preceding.

There are messages in your blood. Nature plays a significant role in who you look like. You look like your ancestors. You are a product of your ancestors' story. The goal of this book is to encourage you to look at your story differently. I want you to see hope, and to come along on the journey that Yahweh (The LORD) is taking your family through. I invite you to take a step back, observe the patterns, connect the dots, read in between the lines, there is an expression from your bloodline that is crying out for manifestation. Will You take these pointers to intentionally design and create a Wealthy HOME? If you don't know your story, it is okay. Now it is time to start finding out.

You may know the story of a people. For example, "The great migration of African Americans in the United States from the South to the North", "The migration of the founding fathers of America on the Mayflower", "the migration of Bantu speaking people to West, Central and South Africa", "The forced migration of native American tribes from present Florida to present day Oklahoma", "The current migration of people from the rural areas to the cities". These "generalized stories" are the product of family stories. Amid generalized stories, what is your family story? We are taught the stories of people in school; however, you must learn the story of your family at home. Your family has a story, and this is the story that is being passed down from generation to generation.

You are part of the story; it would take you going back three to four generations. As you observe, you will see the hidden messages in the blood. You will hear the sound in your blood that has been crying out for expression. You will understand why you do what you do. You will understand why you feel what you feel. You will feel purpose. I encourage you to start on this journey. You will find out a lot of fantastic things. For example, you may not know that one of your ancestors was a teacher, but you just have the gift of teaching, or you are able to effortlessly communicate concepts in a way that people can understand very well. Sometimes you find yourself attracted to a certain profession or role. It will be interesting to see that profession or role up and down the bloodline. That profession is the "oil well" of the family. These professions and/or roles will produce a lot of rewards with little to no effort. The blood speaks.

On this journey, you will discover a lot of wonderful things about your story. Say hi to your story, that is, your history. As you go down the generations, you will discover that your father, mother, uncle, aunt, cousin, and the entire family lineage connected by blood all possess skills in a particular sphere or niche. I encourage you to go even one more generation to confirm the skills of your grandfather, grandmother, granduncle, or any other relative of the grand order. I encourage you to begin your investigations into their professions. Look closely at their strength and areas where they really prospered. You will be amazed at the line that you can draw through all these people. In some families, everyone just picks up an instrument and plays them better than their peers.

> *Take a moment to think through those you know that are still living and start writing what may be common to each of them. Then ask questions from family members that are still alive.*

Most times we go through life looking for purpose.

We look to understand what we need to do. "What I am good at" is one of the responses. You may say that you are multi-talented, true. What that tells me is - over the generations different skills have been honed, but there is one skill that is predominant. Once you discover the "one skill" and you hone it, it would bring greater reward with the least effort. This is true because generations have honed it and the baton has now been passed to you for polishing.

Pay close attention as it is particularly important for you to not only know what your family is good at, but also use that information as a guidepost to number our days and apply our hearts to wisdom. The sages got this knowledge over the generations and passed it down in the most secure format - via the blood, it needs to be passed down to the next generation via the blood, but most importantly via instruction (documented) so that when the next generation starts, they are not beginning from nothing.

As the preacher said in Ecclesiastes 1:9, "there is nothing new under the sun". What has been will influence what will be, and what is today is a product of our history. History continues to repeat itself, whether your family is advancing, stagnating, or regressing. Say hi to your story! It's time for you to go on this journey to understand the story of your family. That wonderful story that is yours begins today. If we go back in time, a couple of our ancestors lived on earth as farmers. A couple of years later they were possibly tools and die-makers.

A couple of years later merchants and industrialists, and now we have found ourselves in the 21st century going to space. One of the things that we do today would not have been possible if we didn't learn from the past generation and improve on what was laid as a foundation of wisdom. Our ancestors honed their skills. They became the best at what they did and then they passed it down to us.

I encourage you to pay it forward by saying "I will be the best at my craft, I will be the best in words and in deeds." A lot of people go through life not knowing what they are to be or do. The surprising thing is those answers are embedded in your blood. The blood carries deoxyribonucleic acid (DNA). This DNA contains information about behavioral patterns, facial features, and skills. It all begins with where we come from. The scripture shows that to gain a heart of wisdom (knowledge/ability to solve problems) we need to "number our days" or the "days numbered in our family".

We need to say *Hi (salute) to our story*. You need to take the time to look back for you to understand what forward looks like. Your family has survived from the beginning of time. Everyone can trace their genealogy to a place on the earth at a particular time. The memories of things that happened in that place are stored in the blood. This in turn is passed down from generation to generation. It has been medically proven that trauma is passed from one generation to the other. In your family, you may have experienced trauma and your ancestors may have experienced trauma. As you go through life, you will process the traumas differently and reposition yourself for a better and brighter future when you number your days.

Lewis, Leach & Wood-Robinson wrote in "Usually *in the Nucleus*", "Genetic material including genes and DNA, controls the development, maintenance, and reproduction of organisms. Genetic information is passed from generation to generation through inherited units of chemical information (in most cases, genes). Organisms produce other similar organisms through sexual reproduction, which allows the line of genetic material to be maintained and generations to be linked. Through reproduction, organisms in a species maintain a 'bank' of genetic information that links individual members and successive generations. Variations in characteristics, such as skin or hair color, are results of the population containing a range of genetic information for specific characteristics."

Lewis, Leach & Wood-Robinson continued stating, "Characteristics that are not seen may be carried in genetic information (recessive) by individuals and can be passed on. This means that offspring may display characteristics different from their parents. The characteristic that is observed may be controlled by a few genes. There are many possible combinations of genes from both parents. The characteristics of the offspring need not be an intermediate of the two parents. Organisms have genetic material that contains information for the development of characteristics. This material passes from one generation to the next through reproduction. All plants and animals are made up of cells where the genetic material can be found in the form of genes and chromosomes."[11]

You may have the following questions:
- Who or what did my ancestors look like?
- What skills did they have?

- How did we even get here as a people?

These are all valid questions that need to be explored in each family. The answers to these questions start with looking in the mirror. Your ancestors had the same resemblance and most likely were very skillful in the things that you are skillful in. Genetically speaking, in the blood is the appearance (resemblance) and the craft (the skill) of one's ancestors. In the medical field, doctors ask questions about one's family history because it has been proven that DNA (genetic material) is passed from parents to offspring. Some families are blessed with long life, others with quick intuitive thinking. Taking the time to document these findings can help you build on the achievements of the past within the brief time that we all have on earth.

In various science journals, there is a raging debate on "Nature vs Nurture". The nature side of the debate argues that a child's destiny is determined by his or her own genes and nothing else. The nurture side of the debate argues that a child's destiny is determined by the environment where the person grew up in. Both arguments are equally valid but instead of looking at it through the lens of "destiny", let us look at it through the lens of behavioral patterns. We know that we are a product of the choices that we make. These choices are influenced by our genetic makeup and what we accept from our environment.

Galatians 4:1
"Now I say that the heir, as long as he is a child, differs nothing from a servant, though he be

lord of all; But is under tutors and governors until the time appointed of the father." (KJV)

Nature and nurture play a very important role in understanding the journey that our families are going through. You might belong to a family of singers but might not be interested in singing or do not sing because of something that happened while you were younger. It may be because of wrong words spoken by peers or family members speaking negatively of the budding artist's ability. This negative influence could lead to the person charting a new course in another profession and shutting down the "ancient well". On the other hand, a person can find themself in a terrible situation growing up like war or famine but still flourish in a trade that has made the family successful for years without even knowing it. The information passed down in our bloodlines has the potential to help us "succeed" in life. Now that we know this, it is imperative that we take a deeper look into our history or better still we say Hi to our Story. How do you say **Hi to your story?**

You start by reaching out to who you know. This can be your parents, grandparents, great grandparents, uncles, aunts, and cousins. Next, you create a family tree and start documenting what you know from those that you have been in touch with. Usually, a lot of family members may not be interested in "talking" because of one thing or the other that happened in the family, but there will be members of the family that are willing to share. As you listen to "family stories", two key questions are important to ask. These questions are found in the story of Samson's birth. An angel visited his parents to announce the birth of the child. During the visit, Samson's father (Manoah) asked the angel a question.

Judges 13:12
> *"Then Manoah said, Now let your words come true. What shall become customary for the lad and his doing?" (Interlinear Scripture Analyzer)*

The family questions are:
1. How did they conduct their lives (behavioral pattern)?
    The three sample questions below may help you process your thoughts:
    a. Are they people that are good with money/industrious people?
    b. Are they warriors that fight for justice?
    c. Are they people that live quietly or do they talk a lot?
2. What was their profession?
    This is particularly important especially if the relative(s) excelled in it. For example:
    a. Are they farmers and/or food processors?
    b. Are they accountants, tax advisors or involved in international business?
    c. Are they clergy, politicians, or government administrators?

In some cases, family members may need to huddle together and appoint a "family scribe". This is the person that would oversee the documenting and passing on of the family stories/heritage. You may also take on the responsibility of becoming the family scribe. It is important to document stories of perseverance and how the family overcame obstacles through the generations. Trust me, these same challenges would repeat themselves in the future, albeit in another way.

If these things are taught to the next generation, they will be well prepared to be overcomers themselves. If you already have a well-documented family tree, congratulations! Make sure that you have the two-family questions answered for as many relatives as possible (as stated in Judges 13:12).

After you have properly documented the above information for every member of the family that you know, take some time to look through the generations to see if you can find any patterns. Usually, you will see a couple of common threads that run through the family line. For example, music could be a theme in your family, or it could be woodworking, dancing, inventors, government, teachers, or runners. These themes are the fruits of seeds that were sown somewhere in the family line. **Say "Hi" to your "Story".** We must nurture what has been put in our families to create a better expected end.

Thoughts to consider:

- Have you created and documented your family tree?
- If yes, do you see trauma or have you seen hope from your family stories?
- If yes, have you spoken to the elders in your family about the future of the family?
- If yes, have you documented your family migration stories and the reason for migrations?
- What is the "oil well" in your family? An "oil well" is a certain line of work that the family has consistently prospered in.
- It is time to Build a Wealthy Home.

Chapter Four

Hope in your Story

D on't wait to take that opportunity but dare to create one. ~ iPen'20

City of Kigali in Rwanda. Picture from Bespoke.[14]

> Job 14:7
> *"For there is hope of a tree, if it be cut down, that it will sprout again, and that the tender branch thereof will not cease. Though the **root thereof wax old in the earth**, and the stock thereof die in the ground; yet through the scent of water, it will bud and bring forth boughs like a plant." (KJV)*

Job 14:7

*"For there is an expectation for a tree: If it is cut down, then it may rejuvenate again, and its young shoots may not be halted. If its **roots grow old in the earth**, and its trunk-base dies in the soil, At the scent of water it shall bud, and it will produce harvest branches like a plant."* (CLV)

Let me rephrase this scripture.

*Your family tree has an expected future. Your roots are strong on the earth (**Say Hi to your Story**). At the scent of water (wealth - education, experience, purpose, wisdom, value creation) your family tree will blossom on the earth and produce mighty nations (generations).*

You have said **Hi to your story**. You have acknowledged your family story. You have saluted the patriarchs and matriarchs in your family. Let us look forward to what our families will become. The call to build your family starts with you.

Jeremiah 1:11:
*Then the word of Yahweh (The LORD) came to me, saying, what do you see Jeremiah? And I answered **I see an almond tree-branch**.* (CLV)

The question here is - What do you see? In earlier chapters, we went through our history. Like a tree, our history (acknowledged and saluted story told by you to the next generation) is the root system. The root systems are beneath the tree. To see the root system, you will need to take time and effort to dig below the surface.

I encourage you to put in the time and effort to look at your family roots. This will help you to understand the history that has been put in the ground. This history, as we understood from earlier chapters, is the foundation for the fruit we see today. Our DNA carries appearance and Skill. The concept of appearance is resemblance and likeness (in form or action). The concept of skill is a profession, career, or work. This connotes education, experience, values, and purpose. These two things merging with the right environment will create a "branch".

The word for branch in Jeremiah 1:11 are from two words Kof —⊖— and Lamed ⌄. Putting them together means "gathering to authority". This speaks of the first expression of the root system. After the seed forms a root in the earth, the first thing that is seen is the stem or "branch" (gather to authority).

In the wealthy home, the next generation "gathers to the authority". They learn from those who have gone ahead of them.

What you see is the product of the root system. What we see in our families is the product of what our history has been. What do you see? Do you just see children, do you just see a father, a mother, a brother, or a sister? Or beyond that, do you see a nation that is being built? When Jacob looked at his children at

70

the time of his passing in Genesis chapter 49, he looked at them and saw beyond their current state. He spoke into three, five, ten, and a thousand generations ahead. He called for who they were and what they would become. The question is - Son of man, what do you see? I want to encourage you to see beyond and create a structure to teach (gather to authority) the next generation.

In most families, the patriarchs and matriarchs of the family do a lot of observation. They watch, they see, they know, and they understand. Based on the current behavioral patterns and the current state of the child, they can project far into the future declaring what the child will become in the future. They can also declare what nation/peoples would come out of that child. Just like Jacob, we are patriarchs and matriarchs of a new generation. Do you see the "branch" in your family? Will you embrace the "branch" (identity) of your family?

This is the concept of seeing in the distance. Looking forward to the future. You can look at the current state of your family and project the next three generations (one hundred and two years). In chapter two, we established that one generation is thirty-four years. In the next hundred and two years, what do you see? Are you preparing the "branch" to bear fruit? You may say, "why should I care about the next generation? Why should I care about the next one hundred and two years?" We see a precedent of this question/behavior in scripture. Hezekiah asked the same question in 2 Kings 20:19. This ultimately led to captivity of this descendants.

2 Kings 20:19:
Hezekiah replied to Isaiah, Good is the word of

71

Yahweh (The LORD) that you have spoken. For he thought, is it not so, if peace and faithfulness shall come to be in my days?

In the above scripture, Hezekiah said *"if it doesn't happen in my generation, I do not care"*. That set the foundation and the precedent for his children to go into captivity. If we do not see into the future and adequately prepare for what is ahead of us, our families might go into captivity. This may sound a little harsh, but it is a reality for a lot of families. Captivity is not something that we should take very lightly. Earlier generations have been through captivity of one form or the other. Their stories are heard across the earth.

Look in Asia, there are stories of captivity. Look in Europe, there are stories of captivity. Look in the Americas there are stories of captivity. Look in Africa, there are stories of captivity. You can also look in Russia, Australia, etc., and you will find stories of captivity. In these stories of captivity, there is a lot of pain and trauma. From the place of captivity some have gone beyond, and harnessed resources for their families to move forward. Most, if not all, have said, "We will never go into captivity again". "This will never happen again."

In some cases, generations down the line return into captivity just like their ancestors. This happens because the ancestors did not adequately prepare the next generation to advance the lessons learned and retain resources (material and immaterial) gained from their experiences. We must prepare the next generation to be strong and do exploits.

*In Jeremiah 1:12, Yahweh (The LORD) responds to Jeremiah that he has **"seen well"**.*

The scripture says that a branch sprouts from a rod of an almond tree. The almond tree is a significant tree in ancient and modern Israel. This tree is the first tree that blossoms in the land. It blossoms in the month of Shevat, speaking of new beginnings. The blooming of the tree signifies that winter is ending. It also signifies the new year of the trees. When you look at your family, do you see the blooming of the branch. Will you look beyond the current state of your family and see the branches that will go over the wall?

A new beginning has begun in your family. A new beginning has sprouted in your family. We must nurture and create the environment for the tree to flourish. Jeremiah saw an almond tree sprouting out of the ground. In other words, this is the beginning of a new beginning. When you look at your family, do you see the beginning of a new beginning? If you are seeing the beginning of a new beginning in your family, you have seen well.

Chapter Five

Act on What You See

The journey to be travelled has been travelled by another before you; find them and gain knowledge for your intended experience. ~ iPen'21

Eko Atlantic is the new hub for business and luxury living in Lagos, Nigeria, and aside from holding the precious Eko Pearl Towers and Eko Corporate Towers, it is also a district full of potential and economic growth.[15]

> Jeremiah 1:12-13:
> *Yahweh (The LORD) said to me, you have done well in seeing, for **I am alert over My word, to perform it.** Then the word of Yahweh came*

to me a second time, saying, what do you see?
And I answered, I see a steaming pot and its
face tipped away from the face of the north.
(CLV)

The world as we know it today is an evolution of its history. At every point in time, there is a constant search for better ways to do things. Human beings are naturally wired to "function". In other words, we are wired to improve on what the earlier generation has done. We are wired to go further. When a new plant buds (shoots up), it stands out from the rest of the plants in the field. A lot of attention is given to the "new". It becomes "popular". The "gardener" gives it a lot of attention. It becomes the center of attraction.

Giving much attention to what is "popular" is nothing new. What is "popular" is an offshoot of what has been before. We can go back a hundred years and see the fads that were in place. Usually, when "new" things arrive on the scene, they come with the wind. Most plants that are not deeply rooted are adversely affected. However, trees with strong roots in the earth withstand the test of time. Irrespective of the winds and the waves of society that come through, we must stand solid as a tree.

Our families must peer into the future, as we saw in earlier chapters, and put together plans to make sure that the next generation does not go into captivity. Let us see beyond the current winds and waves. Are you a tree or a reed? Our families must be as trees planted on solid foundations. Our roots are "old" in the earth, drawing wisdom from the ancients in our families. Reeds are usually tossed back and

75

forth by every wind that blows. A new doctrine comes, it follows; a new fad comes, it follows.

We are creators. The roots of our families are strong on the earth. We are to create new things that others will follow.

The wealthy home is a home that stands the test of time. It is not tossed about by every wave and wind that is out there. It creates movement across the earth. You are a tree planted by rivers of living water. There is a constant flow of life in your veins. Those who have gone ahead of you have laid a great foundation for you to stand on. Your roots are solid in the earth, supplying nutrients to the trunk of the tree (what is seen today). The trunks create support for the branches (the next generation - the extension of the family). These branches supply shade for the birds of the air and the beast of the field. The branches bear the fruits that beautify the trees. This is by design. Are you intentional in designing a wealthy HOME?

There is a Word/prophecy over your family that is yet to be fulfilled in your family. The word is buried in your DNA. It drives the actions within the family. It seeks expression in every generation. It wants to express itself with a touch of excellence. This word can be as simple as:

- We are innovators: We make the world a better place through scientific discoveries.
- We are skilled artisans: We design and build the buildings of the future.
- We are musicians: We release the sound that creates movement on the earth.

- We are newscasters/journalists: we give hope to the world around us.
- We are lenders to many nations.

To understand the Word/prophecy that is over your family, you must first see the **pattern in your roots**. Then you must establish the **support system in your trunks**. The higher the trunk goes the taller the branches will be. How high are you willing to go? How far are you willing to dream? Most importantly, how intentional are you in creating a wealthy HOME? You may be asking yourself this question - What can I do to secure the next generation? It starts with taking a step back and looking into the future. The trends in the past were an indicator of the present. The current trend will also be an indicator of what the future will look like. I want to invite you on a journey to see well and act on what you see.

Growing up in Nigeria in the early 1990s, there were still typewriters in a lot of offices. Many were skilled in using them. There were very few computers in schools, homes, or offices. My parents could have said, "the latest fad is a typewriter, you need to learn how to use them", but they encouraged me and my siblings to learn how to use the personal computer. I'm also grateful to Mr. Tokunbo Onabanjo, the Director of Business Development Education at PPSD (Project Planning and System Development), for introducing me to the personal computer in the early '90s. He opened a cybercafe to teach computer education to young people in the community. He invited me and others to be a part of his television show. The show focused on teaching young people on how to use the computer and its benefits. This show was broadcasted on NTA (Nigerian Television

Authority) on Sundays. I salute you, Mr. Tokunbo Onabanjo.

My parents allowed us to learn to use the personal computer. They looked beyond the typewriters. They positioned and prepared us for the future. Now, the future is here. Computers are everywhere. Those who prepared for it are relevant. Those who did not prepare were left behind. We must look to the future of civilization. What do you see in the next twenty, thirty, fifty or the next hundred and two years? I encourage you to look further.

- What do you see in the next thirty-four (34) years? That is the next generation.
- What do you see in the next sixty-eight (68) years? Can you see further?
- What do you see in the next hundred and two years (102)? Will you see further?

It is important for these foundations to be set up today. Considering the current trend in 2022, in the future there would be a high demand for programmers/coders. Whether you are studying to be a social worker, learning English history, learning to become a musician, dream of becoming a minister, or pursuing your dream of just traveling around the world, it has become imperative to learn how to code. The language of the future is coding. Just like in the 90s, when computers and machine automation were starting to replace a lot of manual functions, so it would be with coding for personalization of automated functions. In the future, there will be a lot of customizations. You might buy a product and would still need to do some form of coding or customization to make it suite your intended purpose.

There are lots of resources out there to use to learn how to code. I want to encourage each person in your family to learn how to code. In the future, artificial intelligence and coding would become normal just like the way computers are normal today. Son of man, what do you see? I say to you, you have seen well. Now, you must be intentional about the word that has been spoken over your family. You need to "gather to the staff". It is time to hear the call to build a wealthy HOME.

> *A wealthy home is where each family member says Hi to their Story (History), learns from those that have gone ahead of them, and increases the reach of the family by applying the wisdom of the ancients.*

There is also a need to teach and prepare the next generation to be the innovators of the future; branches going over the walls, breaking barriers, and producing fruits that beautify the family tree.

Chapter Six

See Beyond the Noise

Mind what you see and hear; for there lies your future. ~ iPen'21

South African embassy Addis Ababa. In 2005 the South African government was awarded land to establish a new chancery. Massa Multimedia Architecture (MMA) architects and a team of South African consultants' along with local counterparts were appointed to realize the project.[16]

> Deuteronomy 15:6
> *Then Yahweh (The LORD) your Elohim (God), He will bless you, just as He **promised** to you. And you will cause many nations to give you securities, yet you yourself shall give no*

*securities. You will rule over **many nations**, but they shall not rule over you (CLV)*

Below is a picture of Deuteronomy 15:6 from biblehub.com interlinear bible:

◀ **Deuteronomy 15:6** ▶

7727 [e]	1471 [e]	5670 [e]		1696 [e]	834 [e]	1288 [e]	430 [e]	3068 [e]	3588 [e]	
rab·bîm,	gō·w·yim	wə·ha·'ă·baṭ·tā	lāk;	dib·ber-	ka·'ă·šer	bê·rak·ḵā,	'ĕ·lō·he·ḵā	Yah·weh	kî-	6
רַבִּ֔ים	גּוֹיִ֣ם	וְהַעֲבַטְתָּ֙	לָ֑ךְ	דִּבֶּר־	כַּאֲשֶׁ֖ר	בֵּרַכְךָ֙	אֱלֹהֶ֙יךָ֙	יְהוָ֤ה	כִּֽי־	
many	nations	and you shall lend to	you	He promised	just as	will bless you	your God	Yahweh	For	
Adj-mp	N-mp	Conj-w	V-Hifil-ConjPerf-2ms	Prep	2fs	V-Piel-Perf-3ms	Prep-k	Pro-r	V-Piel-Perf-3ms	2ms	N-mpc	2ms	N-proper-ms	Conj	

4910 [e]	3808 [e]		7727 [e]	1471 [e]		4910 [e]	5670 [e]	3808 [e]	859 [e]	
yim·šō·lū.	lō	ū·ḇə·ḵā	rab·bîm,	bə·gō·w·yim		ū·mā·šal·tā	ta·'ă·ḇōṭ,	lō	wə·'at·tāh	
יִמְשֹֽׁלוּ׃	לֹ֥א	וּבְךָ֖	רַבִּ֔ים	בְּגוֹיִ֣ם		וּמָֽשַׁלְתָּ֙	תַעֲבֹ֑ט	לֹ֣א	וְאַתָּ֖ה	
they shall reign	not	but over you	many	over nations		and you shall reign	shall borrow	not	but you	
V-Qal-Imperf-3mp	Adv-NegPrt	Conj-w	Prep	2ms	Adj-mp	Prep-b	N-mp		Conj-w	V-Qal-ConjPerf-2ms	V-Qal-Imperf-2ms	Adv-NegPrt	Conj-w	Pro-2ms	

s
ס

Punc.

Deuteronomy 28:12

*Yahweh (The LORD) shall open to you His good treasure, the heavens, to give rain to your land in its season and to bless every work of your hand. **You will obligate (lend to) many nations**, yet you shall not borrow. (CLV)*

81

Below is a picture of Deuteronomy 28:12 from biblehub.com interlinear bible:

◄ Deuteronomy 28:12 ►

Deuteronomy 28 - Click for Chapter

| 776 [e] 'ar-ṣe-ḵā אַרְצֶֽךָ to your land N-fsc \| 2ms | 4306 [e] mə-ṭar- מְטַר־ the rain N-msc | 5414 [e] tā-ṯêṯ לָתֵת to give Prep-l \| V-Qal-Inf | 8064 [e] haš-šā-ma-yim, הַשָּׁמַ֙יִם֙ the heavens Art \| N-mp | 853 [e] 'eṯ- אֶת־ - DirObjM | 2896 [e] hat-ṭō-wḇ הַטּ֗וֹב good Art \| Adj-ms | 214 [e] 'ō-w-ṣā-rōw אוֹצָרֹ֣ו His treasure N-msc \| 3ms | 853 [e] 'eṯ- אֶת־ - DirObjM | 3068 [e] Yah-weh יְהוָ֣ה ׀ Yahweh N-proper-ms | 6605 [e] yip̄-taḥ יִפְתַּ֣ח Will open V-Qal-Imperf-3ms |
| | | | | | | | | la-ḵā לְךָ֩ to you Prep \| 2ms | | 12 |

| 7227 [e] rab-bîm, רַבִּ֔ים many Adj-mp | 1471 [e] gō-w-yim גּוֹיִ֣ם nations N-mp | 3867 [e] wə-hil-wî-ṯā וְהִלְוִ֙יתָ֙ and You shall lend to Conj-w \| V-Hifil-ConjPerf-2ms | 3027 [e] yā-ḏe-ḵā, יָדֶ֔ךָ of your hand N-fsc \| 2ms | 4639 [e] ma-‘ă-śêh מַעֲשֵׂ֣ה the work N-msc | 3605 [e] kāl- כָּל־ all N-msc | 853 [e] 'êṯ אֵ֚ת - DirObjM | 1288 [e] ū-lə-ḇā-rêḵ וּלְבָרֵ֗ךְ and to bless Conj-w \| Prep-l \| V-Piel-Inf | 6256 [e] bə-‘it-tōw, בְּעִתּ֔וֹ in its season Prep-b \| N-csc \| 3ms |

| 3867 [e] til-weh. תִלְוֶֽה׃ shall borrow V-Qal-Imperf-2ms | 3808 [e] lō לֹ֥א not Adv-NegPrt | 859 [e] wə-'at-tāh וְאַתָּ֖ה but you Conj-w \| Pro-2ms |

There are passages in the scriptures that convey promises and/or commandments. We name and claim these promises because we know that Yahweh's (The LORD's) promises will never fail. However, the promise of lending is one that is often overlooked. I want to call your attention to this passage because it speaks of our expected end. I want to encourage you to see beyond the current noise, and act. An athlete performing on the world stage. He/she puts in a lot of effort striving to be crowned the best in the competition. If the athlete ends up less than the best or even as the best, the athlete must still return to train for future competitions if the athlete wants to continue to compete. The athlete is focused and dedicated to the cause. Beyond the current performance, there is a motivating force driving athletes to be the best.

In the same vein, we must strive to be the best in our field. **Your family has been called to be lenders to many nations.** Currently, you may not have any money in your bank account. You may not even have a job. If you are an athlete, you may not have the equipment or coach to train with, but you have a promise. You have a dream, a marching order. Yahweh's (The LORD's) promise to your family is sure and certain.

Will you believe in the promise to lend to many nations?

Psalms 2:8:
Ask of Me, And I shall give the nations as Your allotment, And as Your holding, the limits of the earth. (CLV)

You have not been promised according to the scripture to become the richest man or woman on the planet, the promise is to lend to many nations. You may be looking at the promise and thinking that this seems impossible. You may even be tempted to cloud this promise with your current reality by saying "My bank account is negative right now" or "I don't have money in my bank account and you're asking me to believe that I would lend to many nations?". It is important to note that there is a reason the scriptures say, **"YOU will LEND"**. I like to tell you that this scripture is an invitation to believe what has been promised, and the promise would not fail.

Look beyond the noise in the world. Look beyond the glitz and glamour of what people are striving to achieve. The world out there encourages one to strive to be the richest. The focus is on the contents of the container. To get riches, people burn themselves out in the process. Only to realize that they have lost the most important thing in the process - Building a Wealthy Home. The next generation or the one that comes after spends everything. Very few families across the earth have built wealthy homes. These homes have transferred riches through three to five generations. If you take a deeper look at their business structures, they are lenders and they lend to many nations.

Look beyond the noise and prioritize laying the foundation of a wealthy home. The promise to lend to many nations applies to you too. You may be reading this book saying "I'm older and not able to work. I wish I knew these things when I was young". I want to encourage you not to be discouraged or sad. You are in the best place to build a wealthy home. You have accumulated a lot of wealth (education, experience, purpose, wisdom, and value creation). These are the foundational building blocks of a Wealthy Home. The promise is looking for who would believe and act. The promise is looking for who will set the foundation for generations yet unborn. The promise is saying – "Will you believe, put a strategy in place, and set up a structure so that generations coming after you would lend to many nations?"

How many nations are considered many? Some have suggested, "one", "two", "three" or "four", that's fine. Based on scripture. I would like to propose to you that the number for "many" is forty.

> Deuteronomy 25:3
> *Forty stripes he may give him, and not exceed: lest, if he should exceed, and beat him above these with **many** stripes, then thy brother should seem vile unto thee.*

84

Below is a picture of Deuteronomy 25:3 from biblehub.com interlinear bible:

According to the passage of scripture above, the number forty is considered as many. Inserting the number of "many" back into the Deuteronomy 15:6, the call is to lend to forty nations. What nation are you rehearsing to lend to? I want to encourage you to sit as a family and draft out a document having the forty nations that Yahweh (The LORD) has promised your family. You may be asking yourself, "How would these things be?". You may say, "My ancestors never thought this way, and now I am called to think differently and start a new beginning?". You need a new beginning that sets the platform and the foundation for generations yet unborn.

Isaiah 58:12
And the places deserted for the eon will be rebuilt by you; The foundations of generation after generation you shall raise again; And you will be called, wall-builder of the breach,

Restorer of access-ways for dwelling. (CLV)

I encourage you to look and see beyond the noise of today. You can lay the foundation of many generations. Do you believe that your family will lend to forty nations?

> *The great Martin Luther King Jr. said on April 3, 1968: "I've been to the mountaintop ... I've seen the Promised Land. I may not get there with you. But I want you to know tonight, that we, as a people, will get to the Promised Land."[15]*

Have you been to the mountaintop for your family? Have you seen the promised land for your family? Do you see your family as lenders to many nations? Son of man, it's time to see and document the vision of your family. Now is the time to see beyond your current state, and now is the time to plan for the expected end of your family. Your future is bright and strong. In the next generation - thirty-four years from now, your family could be lending to **one to two nations**. In the next generation after- sixty-eight years from now, your family could be lending to **three to five nations**. In the third generation - one hundred and two years from now, your family could be lending to **ten to thirty nations**.

In the fourth generation - one hundred and thirty-six years from now, your family could be lending to **thirty to forty nations**. The promise is fulfilled according to scripture. This is the goal of a wealthy home. The foundation needs to be laid today.

Generations yet unborn will rise and call you blessed because you laid the foundation of many generations. You became the restorer of the breach. The promise is to lend to forty nations and not to become the richest man or woman on the earth. The promise **is to be a lender and to continue lending.**

Epilogue

The Wealthy Home

Genesis 1:1

In a beginning Elohim created the heavens and the earth (CLV).

Below is a picture of Gen 1:1 from biblehub.com interlinear bible:

◀ **Genesis 1:1** ▶

Genesis 1 - Click for Chapter

776 [e]	853 [e]	8064 [e]	853 [e]	430 [e]	1254 [e]	7225 [e]	
hā·'ā·reṣ.	wə·'êṯ	haš·šā·ma·yim	'êṯ	'ĕ·lō·hîm;	bā·rā	bə·rê·šîṯ	
הָאָֽרֶץ׃	וְאֵת	הַשָּׁמַיִם	אֵת	אֱלֹהִים	בָּרָא	בְּרֵאשִׁית	1
the earth	and	the heavens	-	God	created	In the beginning	
Art | N-fs	Conj-w | DirObjM	Art | N-mp	DirObjM	N-mp	V-Qal-Perf-3ms	Prep-b | N-fs	

The first letter of the Hebrew bible is Bet. The word is the picture of the floor plan of a house- ⌐ . This is not by coincidence; it is by design. The creator of heaven and earth encoded in the scriptures a plan for humanity. This plan starts with the house or home. The house/family is the foundation of any society. The home reflects society at large and society at large reflects the home.

I encourage you to take the journey of self-discovery. Take a step back and look at your home through a different set of lenses. Society has classified, based on certain definitions, who is wealthy and who is not. Wealth as we have explored through the pages of this book has little to do with assets. It has more to do with what has been embedded in our DNA. **You are wealthier than you think.**

Your ancestors have been through a lot. They have written their experiences in blood and passed it down through mannerisms, facial features, and certain types of crafts. You hear things like "In our family we have this type of birth mark, we like to travel, we are musicians ..., the list goes on and on. Your family is crafted by design. To understand this design, you must Say **Hi** (acknowledge, then salute) to our **story**. You need to look back to look forward. There is much wisdom in our roots. Though there might be stories of pain, captivity, trauma and struggle, there are also stories of overcoming obstacles, contributing to the greater good of society, improving processes, and more importantly, passing on to the next generation an improved version of the HOME.

To those reading this book that do not have biological children, you have built a wealthy home. The collective expression of your ancestors is expressed through you. You may think you do not have who to pass on your wisdom to. I have good news for you. Your wisdom will be passed on to the next generation in the form of instruction. In your family tree, you probably have nieces, nephews, cousins, and other close relatives that you can make an impact on. Take some time to help them understand what a wealthy HOME is.

Encourage them to go on this family self-discovery with you as you unlock the treasures hidden in the root system of your family. Nature and nurture play a very important role in understanding the journey that our families have/are going through. It is imperative that we take a deeper look into our history or better still, we say **Hi to our story.**

The journey of understanding a wealthy HOME starts with saying Hi to your story and ends with understanding the expected end - the prophecy that your family is called to fulfill. As you look through your built family tree, see HOPE and resolve within yourself to create a better wealthy home for the next generation to improve on. The previous generation may have stumbled on it just like you but going forward, resolve to structure your wealthy home by design. I leave you with the definition of a wealthy HOME.

> **A wealthy home is a home that harnesses the wisdom imbedded within its rich history to empower each member of the family to solve problems within their sphere of influence.**

- A wealthy home is a home that intentionally creates an enabling environment for all its members to be productive.
- Value creation is at the core of the wealthy home.
- The wealthy home is constantly looking at passing wealth to the third generation. The most experienced (patriarchs/matriarchs) members of the family teach the least experienced members of the family (children under fifteen).

Addendum

A Prophetic Perspective.

This chapter gives a prophetic insight into the days ahead. The destiny of nations are hanging in the balance. We know in part, and we prophesy in part. The prophetic perspectives as written in parables will play out over the next couple of years. These words may be subject to various interpretations based on revelatory understanding. If you choose to interpret these words, I will encourage you to use the patterns in scripture.

The scripture holds true today as in times past. Every prophetic word should be processed through the lens of the scriptures and interpreted accordingly. I encourage you to prayerfully read through these parables but not dwell much on them as they encode blueprints for national dialogue.

To see and understand the expected end, nations must say **Hi to their Story**. We must look beyond the trauma of the past and see the hope of a better expected end. The time has come for the identity of nations to emerge from the ashes of the past and move forward to the glory of the future.

The plane has taken off. The pilots saw "blue skies" and took their eyes off the radar. Unknown to them, they flew into a storm and did not warn their passengers and crew of the "bumpy ride" ahead. Now, everyone must sit tight and turn their hearts towards home. Fasten your belt as the pilot would have to power through the storm.

To those who pilot the houses of the earth, ascend to higher heights, and keep your eyes on the radar. Your expected end is locked and loaded in the flight plan. This is not the time for economic autopilot. Wisdom is profitable to direct. In all your getting, get understanding. Build the house according to the pattern. Be ready for movement. As you move, sow your seed for multiple seasons of harvest. The doors will open at the time of rest. The windows pouring down rain will follow. After which it becomes profitable to activate the autopilot.

The days ahead will be tumultuous for a season till man aligns with the Most High that rules in the affairs of the earth. To some, it is cacophony and to others melody. The expression of melody will come from the conductor himself - The Master of the universe. Many have exalted themselves and said in their hearts, "I will ascend to the heights, I will be as the stars, I will master nature and its forces". Why do the nations rage and the people imagine a vain thing? From the place of exaltation will come the place of exhortation. The nations of the earth roil like a drunkard in the streets, intoxicated with desires as in the days of Noah. Like a dog returning to its vomit, these things are not new.

The sound of heaven has broken through the sound barrier. Portals have opened across the earth ushering in the dawn of a new civilization for Man. LIGHT BE - bring order to the sound coming from the orchestra. Now let us listen to the sound of heaven coming out of the nations. We must be ready to move accordingly. The Horn, though its public perception is insignificant in the orchestra, it is of much importance among the nations. In the past, you have drawn much attention from trade treaties that did not benefit the transit point. Your horn will now be lifted like that of the great Unicorn. No more would you be cast down among the nations of the earth. With it, you will pierce the nations of the earth. In times past you were divided but, in the future, you will take territory with two prongs.

It is written: "Occupy till I come". This also applies to you. Your sound of terror and alarm will now be changed to that of sweet melody. Singing and dancing within your streets again as it was in the days of the great savanna. The place of the great roses blooming at the foot of the mighty hills. Beyond the great river; a people mighty and strong. This is just the beginning of the great realignment. The instruments of the orchestra will be complete. Everyone sounding with equal strength dancing to the beat of the distant drummer. The sounds of the earth in unison with the Most High.

Some have said that the great dragon has reached the ends of the earth with no end in sight but the Most High has raised the islands of the bow. The place of the rising sun must prepare its arrow. Who is he that darkens counsel without knowledge as if that which it has was not given to it? Can the axe boast against he that wields it, or can the pottery say why have you fashioned me this way? You have said, "I made this place. The earth belongs to me to inhabit". How would stewards become masters? Let the straits of Malacca be a barrier for its activities. Let its voice and place be taken and given to another more suitable than it.

Let the mountains that we left desolate quake. It will shake and rattle the tail of the great dragon because it has turned to the effect of the bow. Oh, people of the mountains, arise and thresh with sharp threshing instruments. In the days when the three points split; know that redemption is at hand. Let its voice be heard. Let its place be restored. For you have been weighed upon balances and you have been found wanting. Let the place of Unison be divided by the ram with two horns. For you will be measured with the same measure.

The islands in the shadow of the great eagle crawls looking for the bread to fall from the table. Let the place of paradise be united with its people. Let the voice of the flute bring healing to the lungs of the earth. Breathe, I say breathe. Cover the earth with vegetation and the lands with a great canopy. Let hidden riches in secret places be uncovered. Treasures hidden for the time of discovery. It belongs to you, not those that have come to you.

The great eagle stand strong; the 7th generation has come. It was said that Turtle Island will be restored during your time. Let the stewards of the earth now arise according to the decree of the holy watchers. You will be restored to your former estate as it was in the days of old. Do not remove the ancient landmark which your fathers have set. These are the guideposts giving direction for the one that is to come. You have sat back and watched. Men have looked and not seen the fire prophecies. The heart of Turtle

Island will now beat to the sound of the distant drummer. Your voice will be heard outside you, your face will be seen.

The great Ox has crouched itself down. Its lungs are filled with smoke. It had crouched down in weakness. Laying down in the shadows. The birds of the air have circled over it. The vultures say let us devour; for it is dead. Like in the days past when the angels rejoiced at plunder, you were hunted and brought to the edge of extinction, but I say that your glory will be restored in the days to come. The mighty stones of ancient ruins stand as a testament of visitation. You were visited and hunted from distant shores. The months are at hand when the hunter will be hunted. Arise with strength. A great king will arise from among you. She will lift the tent peg and say that our courts will be extended beyond our shores. For out of the eater will come out sweet and out of the strong will come out meat.

You will be strengthened by the strength of the strong one. The strength of the old will build the new. Your strong foundations uncovered for the earth to see what is possible when man aligns with the Most High. In the days of the lifted tent peg; ships will be sent as they came in the past. I will send rain upon you as it was in times past. I will fill your lungs with my dew. In the days when Jacob wakes from his slumber and Israel from his sleep.

Now arise and clothe yourself, for the day of your redemption is at hand. Once again you will feed and be fed. You will be restored to your former estate as it was in the days of old. Your glory will be fresh within you and your horn exalted as the mighty reem. Arise and thresh the mountains. Say to the islands; it is time to build. Wake up the mines. The treasure houses will be opened again. No longer will your inhabitants want bread. For the produce of the land is meant for the benefit of all; even the king will serve tables.

The king of the North extends his hand beyond. He has said I will restore my glory and be as the land of cedars. In the days to come when his strength wanes, he would look to the prince of the south for alliance. In those days shall the prince of the south battle the dragon. Your sword will be mighty in the earth. As a mighty prince you will prevail in heaven and on earth. Woe to the king of the north. For by means of strength shall no man prevail. You have been a snake in the way, a viper on the path. You have gloried in the stumbling of the horse and rider. Let he that is outside your shores rise to be mightier than you. For your seat will be taken and given to the warriors of old. Gad will inhabit your territory and possess your trade routes. A troop will arise that is mightier than you. Blessed is he that enlarges Gad. He dwells as a lion; he tears the arm with the crown of the head. He provided the first part for himself because a portion of the lawgiver is where he is seated. He came with the heads of the people, he executed justice and judgments in Israel.

Say to Judah, the tree of my planting, your roots have been awakened. Like a mighty Oak, you will rise and tower above the cities of the earth. As a strong tower providing shade for the beasts of the field and the birds of the air. I set a stone in your midst. For in the day's past, it was a stone of stumbling and a rock of offense. Now it is a stone cut without human hands. It is fashioned according to the similitude of the palace. Baked in fire; He emerges with strength. My son is grown up in his youth. Your daughters will be polished as palm trees. Planted by the rivers of waters. Bringing fruits in every season. Your leaves will not wither and whatever you do shall prosper. The glory of Lebanon shall come to you, the fir tree, the pine tree, the box tree, and the mighty oak together, they will beautify the place of my sanctuary and the place of my feet will be made glorious. Israel shall dwell in safety alone.

The fountain of Jacob shall be upon a land of corn and wine; also, the heavens shall drop down dew. Happy are you O Israel, who is like unto you, oh people saved by the Most High. The shield of your help and who is the sword of your excellency, your enemies shall be found liars unto you, and you shall tread on your high places. Blessed are you with these blessings, and according to these blessings are you blessed.

Let it be said that we lived in the days of the children of light. The mighty Eber. The earth is groaning as you groan. Your sound will now be as a roar echoed across the earth. Adding the much-needed trumpet to the orchestra. The mighty conductor called for a pause as a sign in the earth realm. Now let the sound of the trumpet arise and say to the earth realm return to the house, prepare your feet, open the door, exist, and function, connect the voices, draw the sword, bring in the harvest, and build for the days ahead. You will be strong and do exploits. Let the winds gather you from the four corners of the earth. Your staff will smite the rod of the wicked. You will establish a place among the nations, ruling and instructing the affairs of men.

About the Author

Adewunmi Gbogboade is the logistics director for the Global African Business Association (GABA). His background is in engineering, customer service, traffic and transportation systems optimization, supply chain solutions and network capacity analysis. The core of his job function in logistics is demand forecasting and supply chain optimization.

Adewunmi graduated from Lagos State University in Lagos, Nigeria with Bachelors in Electronics and Computer Engineering. He has a Master's degree in Transportation and Logistics Management, specializing in Reverse Logistics from American Military University, West Virginia. For over seven years, he has been teaching and publishing a monthly prophetic perspective, with guidance for the marketplace. He hosts a series called Hebraic Wisdom for Investors. He is married with children.

References

1.https://idioms.thefreedictionary.com/fool+at+forty+is+a+fool+forever

2.Close-up of old-fashioned world map - Stock Freedom - Premium Stock Photography

3.https://today.wayne.edu/news/2021/04/21/answers-in-the-trees-nigerian-engineering-phd-student-searches-for-stormwater-solutions-42446

4.https://extension.colostate.edu/topic-areas/yard-garden/healthy-roots-and-healthy-trees-2-926/

5.Story of cities #5: Benin City, the mighty medieval capital now lost without trace | Cities | The Guardian

6.https://www.merriam-webster.com/dictionary/generation

7.https://www.ancestry.ca/learn/learningcenters/default.aspx?section=lib_Generation

8.https://isogg.org/wiki/How_long_is_a_generation%3F_Science_provides_an_answer#cite_note-3

9.http://www.dept.aoe.vt.edu/~sdross/text/humanhistory.html

10.Ethiopian Bible is the oldest and complete bible on earth (ocl.org)

11.https://www.education.vic.gov.au/school/teachers/teachingresources/discipline/science/continuum/Pages/geneticinfo.aspx

12. Genealogy of the kings of Israel and Judah - File:Genealogy of the kings of Israel and Judah.png - Wikimedia Commons

13. Bespoke Experience – Heaven Retreat

14. New Rising Hotels In Eko Atlantic City | Eko Pearl Towers

15."I've Been to the Mountaintop" | The Martin Luther King, Jr., Research and Education Institute (stanford.edu)

16. http://www.designspaceafrica.com/index/#/south-african-embassy-addis-ababa/

CPSIA information can be obtained
at www.ICGtesting.com
Printed in the USA
LVHW020416170322
713568LV00007B/755